Great
New
England
STORMS
of the
20th
Century

PUBLISHED BY THE BOSTON GLOBE

Patriotic Linnaean Street in Cambridge, Mass. (Jan. 8, 1996).

CONTENTS

INTRODUCTION

New Englanders know about weather extremes. They often amaze us, sometimes sober us, and always prevent us from taking this place for granted. All you have to do is look at some of the incredible storms to hit this region in the 20th century and you realize that living in New England means experiencing virtually every kind of weather imaginable.

And it's not only the range of weather from season to season that's so impressive, but how about going from summer-like to winter-like weather within a day? That's exactly what happened on March 30, 1997, when we were outside enjoying a 63-degree Easter Sunday in Boston and just 24 hours later we were dealing with a storm of heavy, wet snow accompanied by thunder, lightning, and powerful winds. The event became known as the April Fools' snowstorm, but it was no joke to the many Bostonians who lost power and were snowed in for days.

Winter northeasters and blizzards are part of the fabric of New England weather. Old-timers will recall the 1940 Valentine's Day blizzard that paralyzed transportation. Twenty years later, in March of 1960, a vicious northeaster blanketed us in snow and tore deeply into our coastline. And in late February of 1969, what became known as the 100-Hour Storm struck southern New England.

We are vulnerable to powerful northeasters and blizzards because of cold air that frequently comes down from Canada, clashing with moist air that either moves up from the Gulf of Mexico or moves in from the nearby Atlantic Ocean. Never was there a better example than the Blizzard of '78, a storm measured in feet.

I was 29 at the time, and it was my first winter forecasting on Boston television, following three years forecasting in Providence. Ever since I was a little boy I'd been fascinated by weather, especially snowstorms and hurricanes. The Blizzard of '78 seemed to combine all of my fascinations into one.

Outside of New England, many people are aware of the severe winter weather we experience, but they think we have a cakewalk the rest of the year. Nothing could be further from the truth. Hurricanes, tornadoes, and floods have all left their marks on this region. In fact, the greatest natural disaster ever to strike New England was a hurricane.

Known in its day as the Great New England Hurricane, the hurricane of 1938 struck when weather forecasting was in its infancy. On the morning of Sept. 21, most people didn't have a clue that hours later they would be fighting for their lives —about 600 of them losing the battle as a huge storm surge inundated the south coast of New England and put downtown Providence under water.

The 1950s saw New England hit by a series of hurricanes — Carol, Edna, Connie, Diane — and something else that many around here thought impossible: a major F5 tornado. It struck on June 9, 1953, and remains among the 20 most severe tornadoes ever to hit the United States.

I'm most concerned about tornadoes because they can form in minutes. At least with hurricanes, satellite technology and computer modeling let us give you time to prepare. Given that Atlantic hurricane cycles can be active for 20 to 30 years and the most recent activity began in 1995, New Englanders must continue to be on their toes.

With so much new construction along our coastline, the potential for serious damage is higher than it has ever been. And since the last major hurricanes to strike us were Carol and Edna in 1954, many younger people may falsely believe it can't happen here. I'll say it again: Almost anything can happen in New England, including events that are completely unique.

Such was the case in late October 1991. Known at the time as the "No-Name Storm" and later as "The Perfect Storm," this pre-Halloween horror caused massive coastal damage and beach erosion, and was the result of the interaction of three separate powerful weather systems.

In the pages ahead, vivid photos and stories will take you back to these and many other 20th-century events with a newfound respect for the power of Mother Nature and the uniqueness of this place we call New England.

–HARVEY LEONARD, WCVB-TV
co-chief meteorologist, Boston

Fenway Park, April 1, 1997.

SNOW

More than any other weather event, snowstorms have defined New England.

The infamous Blizzard of 1978 may be the one that gets the most attention, but we haven't forgotten the many other snow days this region has experienced in a century that began with powerful, ship-wrecking gales and bone-numbing cold. Events that caused mayhem number in the hundreds, and the "big ones" include holiday blasts such as the paralyzing 1940 Valentine's Day blizzard and a memorable New Year's Eve in 1962, when Maine wasn't partying so much as digging out from a three-day storm that deposited 46 inches.

Parts of New England recorded 3-foot snow drifts in May (yes, May) of 1945 and central Massachusetts saw 4 feet pile up during a single storm in March of '47. Snow isolated Cape Cod in February of 1952, battered central and southern New England in January of '61, and fell for more than 100 consecutive hours during February of '69. March of '93 is remembered for a "Super Storm" that resembled a winter hurricane. And still, Bostonians were caught off guard by a record-breaking April Fools' snowstorm — 25.4 inches in Boston over two days — in 1997.

We should know by now that snow is inevitable in New England. Luckily, though, the white stuff doesn't just make memories, it also makes great pictures.

Downtown Scituate, Mass., in January 1996.

1888

(MARCH 11-14) Yes, we know it's not a 20th-century event. But the grandfather of blizzards, nicknamed the Great White Hurricane of 1888, deserves mention as a 20th-century reference point. It began as a gentle rain on March 11 and quickly turned to snow. Winds gusted to 80 miles per hour and the temperature ranged from zero to 40 below. The blizzard ended three days later, leaving in its wake 400 dead and hundreds of destroyed marine vessels from Maine to Virginia. Many people disappeared in 30-foot snowdrifts; thousands suffered everything from exhaustion to amputation of frostbitten limbs. Elevated trains stalled for hours and cab drivers charged as much as $50 a ride. While Bennington, Vt., reported nearly 50 inches of snow, New York City got only 22 inches, but enough to paralyze the city and persuade officials to fund subways and bury utility wires.

1940

(FEB.14) It was not the kind of love note that New Englanders expected. On Valentine's Day, 1940, 14 inches of wet and unusually heavy snow clogged highways and shut down Boston's buses and subway trains. The snow was twice the normal density, weighing nearly 11 pounds per cubic foot compared to 6.2 pounds for average snow. More than 10,000 people were forced to spend the night at North Station and there were reports of babies born in police cars, trains, and taxis, including a set of triplets. Twenty-seven of the storm's 31 reported deaths were due to exposure.

Products of the Valentine's Day blizzard: Sledding on Boston Common (left) and dumping at Boston's Fort Point Channel (far left).

1945

(MAY 10-11) It's never too late for the white stuff in New England. A freak snowstorm on May 10 and 11, 1945, wreaked havoc in Vermont, New Hampshire, and Maine, damaging fruit trees and knocking down telephone lines. Snowfall swirled into 3-foot drifts in some states. Two highway deaths were attributed to the storm.

1947

(FEBRUARY-MARCH) The winter of 1947 was a jackpot for skiers, with a string of weather in February and March that really piled up the powder. One storm reportedly lasted 16 days and is credited with depositing some 4 feet of snow in central Massachusetts.

May in Maine? Telephone-pole carnage along a Biddeford road (left) in 1945.

1952

For Cape Cod residents, a major pile-up of snow at home in Chatham (above)
and on the main road out of town (right).

(FEB. 27) In one of the worst storms in Cape Cod's history, a northeaster
that brought 20 inches of snow virtually paralyzed the area on Feb. 27, 1952.
Communication to Nantucket was cut off entirely, thousands lost electrical
power, and gusts of 50 mph piled up drifts ranging from 4 to 8 feet that
trapped scores of motorists. Boston, with 6 inches of snow, and Providence,
with about 3, got off lightly, but rush-hour traffic in Providence was still
snarled for hours. At least 10 died from accidents or overexertion throughout
New England. It was the third northeaster to hit the region in 10 days.

MEET THE
Meteorologist

In 1925, Edward Burton Rideout of Arlington, Mass., became the first radio weather forecaster in the United States. Better known as E.B. Rideout, he did daily broadcasts from WEEI in Boston for 38 years, retiring in 1963. Since we couldn't ask this late legendary weatherman to reflect on great New England storms of the 20th century, we consulted his professional descendants. Here and throughout this book, you'll meet men and women whose job it is to predict New England's unpredictable and most extreme weather. All we can say is, better them than us.

Bob Copeland
RETIRED (AND PAINTING) IN NEW HAMPSHIRE

I was a graduate student at the Massachusetts Institute of Technology in March of 1956, when Greater Boston was clobbered by several major snowstorms. The biggest of these was a classic northeaster that moved up the coast and grounded the Greek freighter Etrusco on the South Shore of Massachusetts near the Scituate Lighthouse. Although the Weather Bureau snow measurement for the storm was only 7 or 8 inches, the snow was very wet and blowing horizontally, so the net effect was 8- to 12-foot, meringue-like drifts. Logan airport looked like Antarctica.

1956

In fashion in March of 1956: Clearing windshields (above) and covering up with a classic knitted hood (left).

January 1958, traffic on Chandler Street in Worcester Mass. More snow came in February, when a blizzard hit the region with accumulations of up to 33 inches.

1958

Why doesn't The Globe use "nor'easter"? All the other media outlets do.

What to call these cyclonic storms that raise havoc along the East Coast of the United States and Canada, especially during the fall and winter, with heavy winds off the ocean from the northeast, is hardly an idle matter to many weather-wise New Englanders. Why, some ask, would New England natives accent an "r" in pronouncing a word when in almost every other instance you can think of (hahbah, cah, etc.) the "r" is idiosyncratically missing? The Globe's stylebook takes its cue from vehement opinions expressed in an article written by staff reporter Jeff McLaughlin in 1991.

"New England mariners will say 'noth'easter' and sometimes even 'noath'easter,' " McLaughlin wrote, "but there is never an 'r' sound to be found in the middle of the word." McLaughlin interviewed several old salts in his effort to come to grips with the proper nomenclature. "It really gets my hackles up," said Joseph Garland, who was identified as the historian of the Gloucester fishing fleet. "Unfortunately, you hear it and see it all the time now. It's cutesy at best, probably invented by people who moved here and tried to sound salty."

Above: Pedestrians scurrying through a December 1960 storm in Worcester, Mass.

Right: Man makes his way through that city in March of 1960.

Next page: The blizzards of '60 didn't stop milk from being delivered in the Worcester village of Tatnuck, Mass.

1960

In January, a car abandoned on Route 128 near Canton, Mass.

1961

(JAN. 19-20) Massachusetts' favorite son, John F. Kennedy, was due to be sworn in as president when a howling blizzard roared through New England on Jan. 19, 1961, dropping more than a foot of snow in spots and stranding travelers who had hoped to make it to Washington, D.C., for the ceremony. Thousands more, however, were happily gifted with the opportunity to view the inauguration on television because their schools, industrial plants, and business offices were shut down. The Boston subway system managed to operate but the Celtics game was cancelled when the team couldn't make it home from Philadelphia. Hardest hit was Norfolk, Conn., with 23.7 inches. Fifteen deaths were recorded. President Kennedy was sworn in on Jan. 20 in 8 inches of snow. The storm was the first of three bad ones to hit the region that winter.

In February, benches buried at the Worcester Common.

(FEB. 4) In 1961, New England was enduring its bitterest winter in more than 40 years when a ferocious northeaster whirled into the region on Feb. 4, bringing gale-force winds (39-54 mph according to the National Weather Service) and snow that reached 18 inches in some places. The stinging snow and sleet resulted in widespread power failures, burst water mains, perilous fire conditions, awesome tides, clogged highways, zero visibility, and isolated communities.

1962

(DEC. 29-31) One of the worst blizzards in New England's recorded history came with gale-force winds that piled as much as 46 inches in parts of eastern Maine and 30 inches in Vermont.

Bruce Schwoegler
**VETERAN BOSTON
BROADCASTER AND
CO-FOUNDER OF MYSKY
COMMUNICATIONS INC.**

My broadcasting baptism-under-fire was a record-long snowfall, more than 100 hours, in February 1969. Back then tools were fewer, and you had to analyze weather maps from scratch to develop future scenarios.

Weather has changed the outcome of wars, the spread of pestilence, your commute time, and when the dog gets walked. And it is here, in New England's weather factory, where nature's elements work overtime. Summer storms, winter thaws, sweaty steam baths, and nostril-pinching dryness are but a few products from an assembly line that features mountains and cold to the north and ocean and heat to the south. The mix is volatile, the outcome unsure, the impact immense.

1969

On Morrissey Boulevard, Boston College High School students align to combat a major February snowstorm.

In February of 1969, slow going for a snowbound train in Gloucester, Mass. (right) and two stylish travelers on a clogged street (far right), exact location unknown.

(FEB. 24-28) New England had barely dug out of a huge storm on Feb. 9 when a severe and slow-moving snowstorm arrived on Feb. 24, 1969. Four days and several hours later the flakes finally stopped falling. Mount Washington got 99 inches of snow. A Portland, Maine, weather forecaster warned residents that "unless you're 5-feet-2 or over, you're in trouble." Boston was buried under 26.3 inches of snow; towns like Ipswich, Manchester, and Peabody, Mass., had to cut away 10- to 15-foot drifts on highways before travel could return to normal. The storm shattered records. This time, however, many had heeded advance warnings and stayed off the roads; Massachusetts authorities mobilized more than 2,000 pieces of snow removal equipment and kept traffic mostly flowing. Forty deaths were reported.

(DEC. 26-29) Vermont governor Deane Davis was stranded in Massachusetts when he declared much of his state a disaster area due to the latest December 1969 snowstorm. This one dumped nearly 3 feet of snow in Burlington; thousands were without power, roads and airports shut down, and snowmobiles were enlisted to deliver emergency supplies. Severe flooding ensued.

Is it true that no two snowflakes are exactly alike?

According to "Funk & Wagnalls New Encyclopedia," every snow crystal is unique in its precise configuration because of the infinite variability of weather conditions. One of the most exhaustive collections of snowflake photographs was published in 1931 by the American Meteorological Society. Called "Snow Crystals," the book displayed an astonishing variety culled from 5,150 snowflakes photographed by a reticent Vermont scientist named Wilson Alwyn Bentley (1865-1931), who spent his entire life on his farm in Jericho.

What makes a snowstorm a blizzard?

The National Weather Service definition of a blizzard no longer requires that temperatures drop below 20 degrees. In Boston, the agency considers any snowstorm that reduces visibility to a quarter-mile or less for three hours or more a blizzard. A severe blizzard is one with temperatures below 20 degrees.

How many inches of snow are equal to an inch of rain?

On average, 10 inches of snow is equivalent to 1 inch of rain.

1978

(FEB. 6-7) Whenever a snowstorm rolls into New England, it is always measured against the same yardstick: the Blizzard of '78. The mega storm piled 27.1 inches of snow in a 32-hour, 40-minute burst, including a 24-hour stretch when it dropped at an inch per hour. Snowdrifts reached 16 feet — many people couldn't get out their front doors. There was more than snow to battle. There were howling winds: 70 mph in Boston and 100 mph on nearby Plum Island. Tides rose 20 feet above normal and sucked entire neighborhoods into the sea. New Englanders had anticipated a big snowfall — days earlier meteorologists were predicting "a storm of historic proportions" — but not the huge amounts of white stuff that landed on thousands of motorists trying to get home from work on Monday afternoon, Feb. 6. Many of those stranded on highways didn't make it home for days, some running their cars to empty trying to stay warm until state troopers evacuated them. Of 54 New Englanders who perished in the storm, 14 died on Route 128 in Massachusetts, most from carbon monoxide poisoning as they awaited help. For days, hundreds of thousands coped without power, shared homes with strangers, juggled dwindling food supplies, and amused themselves by candlelight — nine months later there was a mini-baby boom. Memories of the storm remain indelible, like the sight of interstate highways clogged with abandoned vehicles — 3,500 on an eight-mile stretch of Route 128 alone — or Massachusetts Governor Michael S. Dukakis, clad in a reassuring pullover sweater, on TV calling for patience. Those who lived through that week have never forgotten the harsh lesson in nature's ways, or the mountains moved by neighbors pulling together when it mattered most.

Left: Crossing Boston's Commonwealth Avenue.
Above: Michael Dukakis (in turtleneck) with his storm team.

Kevin Lemanowicz
WFXT-TV, BOSTON, MASS.

Like everyone else who grew up in New England, I remember the Blizzard of '78. We stayed home from school for a week with our parents. We lived in Moosup, Conn., and the state had been shut down, so traveling was prohibited. The "big kids" jumped off the roof of our two-story apartment complex into the immense snowdrifts below. When we opened our back door, we had to tunnel through the snow to find sunlight.

Steve Cascione
WPRI-TV/WNAC-TV,
PROVIDENCE, R.I.

It's been about 30 years since the Blizzard of '78, but to this day all we have to do as meteorologists is mention the "b-word" in a weather forecast and we can clear most supermarket shelves of milk and bread in a few short hours.

My fellow Ocean Staters will never forget two things about the Blizzard of '78: the snow totals were a little off, and the kitchen shelves were a little empty.

Route 128 in Massachusetts (February 1978).

Above: Climbing the streets of Boston's Back Bay (Feb. 10, 1978).
Right: Skiing the streets of downtown (Feb. 6, 1978).

The Boston Globe

Worst storm of century

17 die . . . record high tides . . . up to 4 feet of snow . . .
winds gust up to 125 mph . . . highway traffic banned

Just as the storm of 1978 created memories, it also destroyed a few, like the amusement pier at Old Orchard Beach in Maine, Motif #1 in Rockport (which would later be replaced), and the Peter Stuyvesant riverboat next to Anthony's Pier 4 restaurant in Boston.

Don Kent, a now-retired meteorologist for WBZ in Boston, began work at 5 a.m. on Monday, Feb. 6. He had been tracking the storm since the previous Friday. Even without today's sophisticated weather radar technology, he knew something big was on its way. "The producers kept saying, 'Hey Kent, how much are we going to get?' I could only say it was the biggest storm I'd ever seen," said Kent, who is now in his 80s and lives in New Hampshire. "At 11 o'clock, I went on the air and said, 'This storm is going to be measured in feet, not inches.' By 7 o'clock on, it was like a whiteout."

March 1984: Massachusetts motorists pitch in to move a bus.

(MARCH 13) Cross a hurricane with blinding snow and you will get a sense of the storm that blasted through southern New England on March 13, 1993. Boston shut down as hurricane-strength gusts and heavy snow bombarded the region and wind-whipped tides rose 4 to 12 feet above normal. By the early evening, the 135-foot-high Tobin Bridge, which stretches over the Mystic River, was shut down due to the high winds. The snow — measuring nearly a foot at Logan Airport — was enough to make the winter the snowiest since 1977-'78, the year of the legendary February blizzard. Yet New England got off easy compared to the rest of the East Coast. The killer storm dumped a record 15 inches of snow on Birmingham, Ala., and spawned 50 tornadoes before it moved northeast through Washington and New York and into New England.

1993

A UPS driver tripped up by Boston's "Super Storm" of '93.

(JAN. 7-8) Coastal communities held their breath when forecasters warned that an impending snowstorm could reach 1978 proportions. But the Blizzard of '96 was only a weak cousin of its famous predecessor when it finally reached New England on Jan. 7. Parts of Boston's South Shore did get 2 feet of snow but the tides were not overly high and only minor damage was caused. By contrast, New York City got walloped with as much as 30 inches, and many governors from Kentucky north declared states of emergency. The fierce system was ultimately blamed for at least 47 deaths.

1996

Just another January snow day in Squantum, Mass.

"Thomas Jefferson said there wasn't as much snow as when he was a boy. That's what everybody says. If that were so, there wouldn't be any snow anymore."

ROBERT LAUTZENHEISER, retired Massachusetts state climatologist

1997

(MARCH 31-APRIL 1)
Mother Nature has a wicked sense of humor. Just when New Englanders thought it was safe to put away the shovel, snow began falling on Monday, March 31, 1997, and by the next day — April Fools' Day — it had reached 25-plus inches in Boston and as much as 36 inches in the rest of the state. The drifts were no joke for motorists stranded on Route 128 and for Boston commuters. Most Bostonians took the storm in stride, — it had been a mild winter — but the late-season snow cut off power to thousands of people, damaged trees at the Arnold Arboretum in Jamaica Plain, and sheared off the top of the USS Constitution's foremast. A total of three snow-shoveling deaths were reported in Rhode Island and Massachusetts. By the next weekend, brilliant sunshine had erased most traces of the April Fools' blizzard.

Below: A car parked at Harvard University.

Right: A commuter in Boston's Back Bay.

MEET THE
Meteorologist

Barry Burbank
WBZ-TV, BOSTON, MASS.

On a 63-degree Easter Sunday in 1997, I was predicting a major snowstorm leading into April Fools' Day. Boston viewers called to say that the forecast must be some sort of a joke. But the next day, rain mixed with sleet and then a blizzard ensued.

Fast forward to two days before Christmas that same year: I told my audience that 1 to 3 inches along the Mass. Pike and 3 to 6 inches for northern Massachusetts would be a nice white gift. But a seemingly innocuous setup blossomed into 6 to 8 inches per hour over northern Massachusetts and southern New Hampshire, with amounts totaling 14 to 24 inches.

That's why forecasting New England weather accurately is the ultimate challenge; the region's topography and proximity to the ocean can mean as many defeats as triumphs. In 1997, I had a taste of each.

Fenway Park, April 1, 1997.

ICE

It looks so magical when it's hanging from the eaves and gutters in translucent cones, or turning barren trees into something out of a sparkling glass menagerie.

But ice has a dark side, too. It's been known to snap branches, down telephone lines, and make roadways impassable — not that motorists born in the Northeast will ever back down from trying.

Over the 20th century, ice storms took their toll on New England in the form of a 1921 November freeze-up in the Worcester area of Massachusetts, slippery January events that made Boston a treacherous commute in 1994, and a 1973 December storm covering western Massachusetts, most of Connecticut, and parts of Rhode Island.

In January of 1998, much of Vermont, New Hampshire, and Maine in particular were hit by two storms that together accounted for one of the most severe ice assaults of the century. The destruction also spread across neighboring upstate New York and Canada. At one point it was estimated that 500,000 customers had lost power, leaving them with no heat, no pumps for their water, and frozen pipes. The fact that miles of transmission lines were brought down by the weight of the ice was a major factor in the massive outage. It took weeks to restore power in some parts of Maine.

That's the dark side of ice.

Old Man Winter? Nope. A statue of Edward Everett Hale in the Boston Public Garden, 1995.

A New England winter ritual: scraping the car windshield.

When did "wind chill factor" first come under consideration by weather forecasters?

Dr. Paul Siple's experimental observations in 1939 at the Antarctica base Little America brought attention to the combined effect of wind and cold on exposed human flesh. The wind chill chart developed by the US National Weather Service, based on temperature and wind speed, is derived from Siple's formula of heat loss from exposed human skin due to four causes: conduction, convection, radiation, and evaporation.

Do birds' feet freeze in cold weather?

According to The Audubon Society's "Encyclopedia of North American Birds," their feet may freeze occasionally, but that type of frostbite is rather rare among avians. Because birds' toes and ankles have tough tendons and a limited supply of nerves and blood, their feet apparently are far less susceptible to freezing than are the fleshier parts of their bodies.

Does water expand or contract when it freezes?

Water expands when its temperature is lowered to 32 degrees Fahrenheit and it begins turning to ice. Because it expands in the freezing process, ice has less density than when liquid. Thus, ice can float on water.

1921

(NOV. 26-29) Roofs, trees, and telephone poles were no match for tons of ice that hit New England during the final week of November in 1921. Massachusetts' Worcester County saw ice up to 4 inches thick in some places, paralyzing towns for weeks before service was restored to outlying areas. The Worcester Telegram reported "an almost impassable chaos of tangled wires, broken branches and uprooted telephone poles." The city lost its fire-alarm system and nearly all communication with the outside world for a few scary days that must have seemed like an eternity.

Out of gas and iced up on Winthrop Beach Boulevard in Massachusetts (March 1923).

1973

(DEC. 16) One of Connecticut's worst ice storms in decades brought trees crashing down throughout the state on Dec. 16, 1973, cutting off power to 250,000 households and businesses. Writing many years later in the Hartford Courant, meteorologist "Dr. Mel" Goldstein remembered that "Pounds of ice accumulated on trees and wires. Gusty winds then snapped those limbs and even entire utility poles ... The lack of electricity created hardship with heating systems being disrupted and pipes freezing and bursting in many homes." With temperatures hovering around zero, people loaded up fireplaces or sought refuge in schools or armories. Eight deaths were attributed to the storm, six from asphyxiation as people tried to stay warm with makeshift heaters. The cleanup bill totaled at least $12.5 million.

What do the weather experts consider the most significant weather events to hit these parts since they started keeping records?

In their book "New England Weather, New England Climate" (University Press of New England; copyright 2003), climatologists Gregory A. Zielinski and Barry D. Keim offer their candidates for New England's Top 10 weather events of the 20th century:

10 • Flooding from two days of rain on Nov. 3-4, 1927.
9 • Blizzard of Feb. 22-28, 1969.
8 • Northeaster on Oct. 20-21, 1996.
7 • The 231-mph wind recorded atop Mount Washington on April 12, 1934.
6 • Worcester Tornado of June 9, 1953.
5 • Ice storm of Jan. 5-9, 1998.
4 • "All New England Flood" of mid-March in 1936.
3 • Hurricane Diane on Aug. 17-19, 1955.
2 • Northeaster blizzard of Feb. 5-7, 1978.
1 • Hurricane of Sept. 21, 1938.

Date ranges above may not match other references, which were compiled from Boston Globe reports.

Admiring the icicles at Harvard's Newell boathouse, Cambridge, Mass., in January 1961.

1994

Never too young for ice fishing, or battling icy elements, at Lake Cochituate in Natick, Mass. (Jan. 17, 1994).

(JANUARY) Sports fans and scandal lovers remember Jan. 6, 1994, as the date that Nancy Kerrigan was clubbed on the knee after a practice at the US Figure Skating Championships in Detroit ("Why, why, why?"). But New England weather geeks also know it was part of a month fraught with snow and ice storms that made a slippery mess of Boston and other parts of the region.

Not skiing, just taking in Maine's sparkling Shawnee Peak in January 1998.

MEET THE
Meteorologist

Tom Messner
WPTZ-TV, VERMONT

For more than 80 hours, the rain fell, freezing onto every surface imaginable. There were intervals of eerie silence, dramatic cracks and crashes of giant tree limbs, and the occasional fireworks of an exploding transformer. That was in the early hours of the January '98 ice storm, when there was still electricity.

I spent two nights on my station's lumpy couch, catnapping between live updates. Home was less than 10 miles away but felt like another time zone. As the storm entered its third day, lifetime residents told the television cameras, "I've never seen anything like this."

But ask a Vermonter about that storm today and you'll hear just as many stories about neighbors arriving with firewood, shelter volunteers reading to children, and farmers milking one another's cows. You'll hear stories that remind you of old-fashioned barn raisings, because that's what New England was, and still is, all about.

1998

(JAN. 5-9) Trees and bushes were lacquered with a translucent and terrible beauty. Inch-thick ice rendered roads impassable. In Bangor, Maine, the horizon was lit up with blue and orange flashes from exploding transformers. New London, N.H., looked like it was hit by a bomb because of the downed power lines across roadways and pines shattered from the weight of the ice. In January of 1998, two of the region's most severe ice storms caused devastation throughout Maine, New Hampshire, and much of Vermont. The first storm hit Jan. 5 to Jan. 9 — some areas had 100 straight hours of freezing rain and sleet. A second, one-day ice storm hit about two weeks later. As many as 500,000 customers lost power for days, leaving them with no heat, no pumps for their water, and frozen pipes. Deaths were reported from carbon monoxide poisoning due to malfunctioning heaters and generators. Many mourned the destruction of so many beautiful trees in their communities. "Every tree that we planted or was in the yard is broken," a New London, N.H., woman lamented to a Boston Globe reporter.

MEET THE
Meteorologist

Joe Cupo
WCSH-TV,
PORTLAND, MAINE

Unseasonably warm and moist air pushed northward in January of 1998. As it approached northern New England it encountered a layer of much colder air that remained glued to the surface. Neither air mass was going to give in to the other.

Power lines and tree limbs weighed down with ice. People drained their pipes and evacuated their homes, not knowing how long it would be before power and heat were restored, or if the restoration would last.

In the midst of the devastation, I met a man at a crowded home improvement store. He'd been waiting all day for a delivery of generators. When I asked him why, he told me he was a hunter and had a large freezer full of deer meat. "Either I get a generator or I go hungry," he said. This gave me a whole new perspective on the ice storm of 1998.

Freeing
up the
power
lines in
Hallowell,
Maine
(January
1998)

MEET THE
Meteorologist

Fred Ward
VETERAN WEATHER-
CASTER, RETIRED (BUT
STILL ANALYZING) IN
NEW HAMPSHIRE

A little-known part of meteorology depends on special weather events, but not blizzards, floods, or hurricanes. These unheralded events affect the lives of many people in ways that can be even more memorable than the big storms. They cause serious accidents and injuries.

In my "retirement," I analyze the weather to help courts decide which party in a dispute is likely at fault. A common weather pattern is very often the culprit: rain turning to snow as the temperature falls, making slush and puddles that eventually freeze and get covered with more snow.

My weather memories are of just such events, including Jan. 23, 1992, when I had 24 cases, largely falls and auto accidents. The day was mostly rainy, with the temperature rising into the 50s. But there was a short, severe ice storm before the mild weather arrived. It was just another regular winter event with dire consequences, and it was likely not even forecast.

In New London, N.H., a landscape reshaped by ice (Jan. 10, 1998).

Wind and snow are frequent companions on the Auto Road leading to the Mount Washington Observatory (inset).

WIND CHILL

MOUNT WASHINGTON, N.H.

"It was scary. It was a scary, scary ride." That's how John Bruni remembers his trip in March of 2006 to the highest peak in the Northeast. He and six other curious individuals were tucked inside a snow tractor plowing its way yard-by-yard through a blinding blizzard. They were participating in an educational seminar sponsored by the Mount Washington Observatory (www.mountwashington. org) and were getting exactly what they signed up for: subzero cold, whiteout conditions, hurricane-strength wind gusts, and a chance to experience what often is described as the "home of the world's worst weather." Their trip leader was Peter Crane, director of programs for the observatory, a private, nonprofit organization that operates a year-round weather research facility at the summit.

Bruni had wondered what it was like on the 6,288-foot summit in winter. He got his answer in no uncertain terms. The wind was blowing hard, and from inside the tractor they could see nothing outside. At times, neither could the driver. So they stopped. They sat. They waited, until the visibility improved so they could at least see the edge of the road, where the cliff begins. One of the things that makes Mount Washington unique is its wildly unpredictable and extreme weather, the result of its geography and topography. This combination of factors makes the mountain an ideal place for the weather observatory — and makes its summer and winter educational seminars so enticing.

It's always an adventure when you summit Mount Washington. "It's like going to the beach in a storm," Crane said in explaining the lure. "People can experience the extreme without having to travel thousands of miles. On Mount Washington, they can sample the elements [as part of a guided trip] and no one gets hurt."

Situated halfway between the Arctic and the equator, and near the border of North America and the Atlantic Ocean, Mount Washington is at the confluence of three major storm tracks: coastal (such as northeasters), Appalachian (sometimes fetching moisture from the Gulf of Mexico), and Canada and the Great Lakes (often propelling cold air). The conflicting dry, humid, hot, cold, and maritime air masses, pushed along by prevailing westerly winds, barrel up the mountain slope and collide with an area of lower pressure that can yield cool, cloudy, wet, and windy conditions — often tallied in extreme degrees.

Since 1932, observatory staff have monitored these elements. In 1934, they recorded the world's highest surface wind speed at 231 miles per hour. Put in perspective, a Category Five hurricane has sustained winds greater than 155 miles per hour. While visitors are unlikely to be blown away by a record wind gust, they likely will struggle against mean wind speeds of 25 miles per hour in summer and 50 miles per hour in winter.

Winds up to 100 miles per hour are common enough in winter that staff and guests vie to join the informal "century club." Although no roster is kept, those who manage to walk the several hundred feet around the observatory deck under their own power — no crampons, no poles — can claim membership. For those who fail, or rather fall flat from a gust of wind, there is the "crawl of shame," also with no official roster.

-PEGGY HOFFMAN, Globe Correspondent

"People are very bold with their e-mails. The most common is, 'Do you guys ever look out the window?'"

ED CARROLL, WGGB-TV, Springfield, Mass.

MEET THE
Meteorologist

Sarah Long
WGME-TV, PORTLAND, MAINE

From Mount Washington Observatory summit log book, Jan. 7, 1998: "It's the ice storm of the millennium. Much of the Northeast is encased in glaze ice and is without power. Mount Washington enjoys a balmy 45 degrees." —Observer

In January at the Mount Washington Observatory we usually experience harsher conditions than those down below. But during the ice storm of '98, it was just the opposite.

While we were basking in tropical air (mid-40s) at 6,288 feet, the Auto Road — our only winter passage to and from the summit — was blocked by a tangled mess of trees downed by ice. Road crews spent three days working to clear a path for the relief crew. Once they arrived, my shift partner and I passed up a ride in the snow tractor to take in the scene step-by-step.

The eight-mile hike down the curvy road to the valley floor was surreal: one moment no signs of ice, then turning the corner to find a glaze covering every surface. It was an eye-opening descent and a reversal of fortunes for those living and working (in my case for a total of four years) at the "home of the world's worst weather."

TWISTERS

AND THUNDERSTORMS

The wind began to switch, the house to pitch, and suddenly the hinges started to unhitch...

No disrespect intended, but that lyric from "The Wizard of Oz" is probably what most coastal New Englanders think of when they think tornadoes. Twisters only happen in places like Kansas, right?

Well, no.

As anyone who grew up in parts of Connecticut or Massachusetts can tell you, tornadoes have done their share of damage in this region, too. In fact, there were more than 60 tornadoes recorded in Connecticut between 1950 and 1994.

One of the most significant events happened on a June day in 1953, when cyclonic winds ripped through communities in and around Worcester, Mass., leaving 94 dead and some 15,000 homeless. Though that twister has no equal in New England's recorded history, people in the area also still talk about tornadoes that hit in 1924, '38, and '73.

In 1979, a fierce funnel cloud touched down in Windsor Locks, Conn. In '86, Rhode Island saw a rare visit by three twisters in the span of a day. And in '95, the Berkshires of Massachusetts were hit by a tornado with 200-mph winds.

Just about anywhere in New England, thunderstorms can roll in swiftly with combinations of rain, wind, and lightning that should never be underestimated. Whole neighborhoods have been leveled and lives uprooted without warning. Yes, it can happen here. It has.

1924

(JULY 17) You don't hear much about the twister that hit Fitchburg, Mass., on July 17, 1924, but it was powerful enough to reduce large brick buildings to rubble. A garage housing four automobiles was moved 80 feet according to one account, with the cars undamaged. The amusement park at Lake Whalom was demolished — not for the last time — and two deaths were reported along with about 25 injuries.

1938

(AUG. 16) It was dubbed the $60,000 Cyclone. The twister that tore through an amusement park in central Massachusetts on Aug. 16, 1938, caused $60,000 worth of damage when it struck as Whalom Park patrons were at the penny arcade, in the dance hall, or camped out at nearby Whalom Lake. The tornado touched down on the Fitchburg line and swept through Lunenburg and North Leominster. Winds toppled part of the park's roller coaster (again) and uprooted trees. Astoundingly, no one was killed and the park owners vowed to rebuild, only to be hit by the 1938 hurricane (page 88) a month later.

1953

Before and after: St. James Road in Shrewsbury, Mass.

"When population density is factored into the tornado occurrence equation, the odds of a person being affected by a tornado are greater [in Connecticut and western Massachusetts] than in any other part of the country, including Dorothy's Kansas."

DR. MEL GOLDSTEIN, WTNH-TV meteorologist

Senator John F. Kennedy amid 1953 tornado rubble in Shrewsbury, Mass.

(JUNE 9) On a stifling spring day, a merciless black funnel of wind unleashed its wrath in central Massachusetts, cutting a swath of destruction 40 miles long through communities from Barre to Southborough. The most powerful and destructive tornado ever to strike New England killed 94 people (revised from an initial estimate of 100), injured about 1,300, and left as many as 15,000 homeless. Just before 4:30 p.m. on June 9, 1953, the distinct silhouette of a funnel cloud was spotted near Petersham. By 6 p.m., the mile-wide F5 tornado had roared through Worcester, damaging at least 4,000 buildings and leaving hundreds out of work. In winds that reached 327 miles per hour, telephone poles were sent flying like darts, houses were moved a quarter of a mile, and cars were tossed like toys. A "Day of Mourning" was declared and President Eisenhower flew in to inspect the devastation. The storm that became known as the Great Worcester Tornado increased pressure to improve forecasting tools.

1973

(AUG. 28) At a truck stop on Route 102 in the Berkshires of Massachusetts, people know that New England's "Tornado Alley" is no laughing matter. On Aug. 28, 1973, the truck stop was creamed by an F4 tornado that blew into West Stockbridge from New York. The storm caused four deaths and injured 10 times that many in the area before it spun itself out.

1979

(OCT. 3) In a scant 15 minutes, three people were killed, some 500 injured, and 40 homes destroyed when tornadoes touched down without warning in central Connecticut on Oct. 3, 1979. A north-moving line of at least three funnel clouds cut a five-mile path from Windsor and Windsor Locks to Suffield. Ferocious, F4-level winds tore through the Bradley International Airport and destroyed the headquarters of the Bradley Air Museum. The roof of an elementary school in Windsor was ripped off — luckily the students had been dismissed early for a teachers' conference. Interstate 91 was shut down midway between Hartford, Conn., and Springfield, Mass. With damages estimated at $200 million, this remains one of the costliest tornadoes in history.

Can you explain the new scale used to grade tornadoes?
The original Fujita Scale was created in 1971 by University of Chicago professor T. Theodore Fujita to rate a tornado's severity, from those causing light damage to catastrophic events. The scale's estimates of destructive wind speeds were revised in February of 2007, and the new Enhanced Fujita Scale also adds damage indicators aimed at refining the categorization of tornadoes.

Fujita Scale
F0: 40-72 mph
F1: 73-112 mph
F2: 113-157 mph
F3: 158-207 mph
F4: 208-260 mph
F5: 261-318 mph

Enhanced Fujita Scale
EF0: 65-85 mph
EF1: 86-110 mph
EF2: 111-135 mph
EF3: 136-165 mph
EF4: 166-200 mph
EF5: more than 200 mph

Aug. 10, 1979: Residents clear debris in Paxton, Mass., where powerful thunderstorms felled trees that killed two people at a Boy Scouts camp.

Oct. 5, 1979: Classic airplanes destroyed by the tornado at Bradley Air Museum in Windsor Locks, Conn.

71

Utility lines
downed by
tornado winds
in central
Massachusetts
(June 1981).

(AUG. 7-8) In less than 24 hours starting on Aug. 7, 1986, three tornadoes struck Rhode Island, a state where glimpsing a twister might otherwise happen once in a lifetime. F2 funnel clouds touched down first in Cumberland, then in Providence during rush hour, and finally in North Smithfield the following morning. Twenty people suffered minor injuries. "Up until this week, we had about one tornado every 80 years," a retired meteorologist told the Associated Press. "But that's during normal conditions. If weather always behaved normally, we wouldn't need forecasters."

1986

The Fulton Building on Stewart Street in Providence, R.I. (Aug. 9, 1986).

Pete Bouchard
WHDH-TV, BOSTON, MASS.

As if our internal demons weren't enough, there's always an audience to put us in our place.

I remember as a young forecaster in Bangor, I saw a raging northeaster coming through the Gulf of Maine. "I don't recommend even trying to go out," I warned. Six hours later, flurries stopped and the sun came out. A week later, I got a letter from a viewer.

"Based upon your forecast, I did not go to work on Tuesday. I missed out on 8 hours of work. Since I make $5/hr., you owe me $40 for that fumbled forecast. I expect prompt payment to the above address."

I felt so guilty I almost sent him the money. Then again, I'm glad I didn't. If I'd gotten into that habit, I'd be broke by now.

Dr. Mel Goldstein
WTNH-TV,
NEW HAVEN, CONN.

At noon on a steamy July afternoon in 1989, I noticed very heavy thunderstorms hovering over the Berkshires. By mid-afternoon, the skies across Connecticut opened up. A series of tornadoes broke out from Cornwall in the northwest corner to Bantam, a section of Litchfield. Beautiful woods were destroyed; downtown Bantam was flattened. Then, the squalls pushed southward with the strongest tornado of all yet to be spawned.

I was in our downtown New Haven studio watching the sky become midnight-dark. On the air, I said to my co-anchor, Mark Davis, "Mark, I have never seen the sky become so dark on a summer afternoon." He said, "Dr. Mel, I have never seen you perspire on TV as you are right now."

The tornado swarm was the longest ever to strike Connecticut.

Thunderstorm damage to a tree at Calvary Cemetery in Brockton, Mass. (May 1996).

76

1989

(JULY 10) When severe thunderstorms spawned several tornadoes (including an F4) on July 10, 1989, amazed residents of Hamden, Conn., saw cars fly through the air and houses blow apart amid blasts of lighting and hail the size of ice cubes. About 200 homes and businesses were destroyed and dozens of people suffered injuries as a result of the extreme weather. At least two were reported killed, one a teenage girl who was struck by a falling tree in Black Rock State Park north of Waterbury, Conn.

1995

(MAY 29) Just as the Memorial Day weekend was winding down on May 29, 1995, a fierce storm and F4 tornado crashed into Great Barrington, Mass., killing three people in a car that was picked up like a candy wrapper and sent slamming into the woods. Dozens more were injured. Winds estimated at 200 mph carved a 15-mile path of flattened forests, downed power lines, and debris-blocked roads across three Massachusetts towns in Berkshire County. "It's like a plane dropped a bomb," a volunteer fire chief told a Boston Globe reporter.

A blown-out home in Great Barrington, Mass. (May 30, 1995).

"My fascination with severe weather had started when I was a young child, so I decided on 'TSTORM' for my New Hampshire license plates. When I came down to visit a Boston TV station on an informational tour, I landed the weekend meteorologist job at age 24 thanks in part to those plates. The news director there realized I was a true weather nerd, not someone who just wanted to be on TV."

MISH MICHAELS, WBZ-TV meteorologist

What's the difference between a tornado and a cyclone?

A cyclone is a low-pressure weather system highlighted by the cyclonic circulation of wind, clockwise in the Southern Hemisphere, counterclockwise north of the equator. The types of cyclone most familiar to New Englanders are hurricanes and tornadoes.

How does the National Weather Service measure wind velocity?

By international agreement, the Weather Service supplies wind speeds which are averages of the speeds measured with an anemometer in the 10 most recent one-minute periods up to observation time. Reports of "wind gusts" represent the top speeds observed in the 10-minute period.

Left: A three-alarm fire started by lightning in Westwood, Mass. (June 22, 1997).

Above: Revere Beach-goers wait out a typical summer thunderstorm in the Boston area.

Right: In Coventry, Vt., a rainbow can brighten the darkest day.

Next page: A June 1997 thunderstorm darkens and blurs motorists' view of the Boston skyline.

What is the origin of the expression, "Red skies at night, sailor's delight; red skies at morning, sailor take warning"?

According to the "Home Book of Proverbs, Maxims and Familiar Phrases," the earliest of many versions of the saying appears in the New Testament. The Gospel of Matthew (16:2-3), written about 65 AD, reads: "When it is evening, ye say, it will be fair weather; for the sky is red. And in the morning, it will be foul weather today; for the sky is red and lowring."

COASTAL
BLASTS

New England is always on the watch for tragic, destructive coastal storms.

They've come as northeasters, hurricanes, and rain-packed southeast gales. They've taken thousands of lives, wrecked countless boats and ships, and reduced waterfront properties to splinters. Towering waves and abnormal tides have stormed across sandy beaches and over walls with such force that picturesque shorelines and hundreds of homes were swallowed by angry seas.

New Englanders of a certain age may remember the historic 1938 hurricane and another nameless-but-notable storm in 1944. Then came Carol and Edna in 1954, Connie and Diane five days apart in '55, Donna in '60, Belle in '76, Gloria in '85, and Bob in '91.

Northeasters have been more infrequent, but still significant: In January 1905, gales caused millions of dollars in property damage with coastal shipping taking a major hit. In April 1911 and April 1950, the winds were particularly severe on Cape Cod and the Islands. In January 1933, beach properties and shipping were again hit hard. And in March 1947, wind-driven tides caused extensive damage between Boston and Salem.

Perhaps most famous these days is the 1991 "No-Name Storm," more popularly known as "The Perfect Storm" after a book and movie of that title. We recall it a little differently from the version with George Clooney. In New England, there's never a need for special effects.

Preparing for 1961's Hurricane Esther, which ultimately didn't live up to the hype, at a Worcester, Mass., barbershop.

Towering waves (right) hit Winthrop, Mass., in April of 1929; beachfront damage (far right) lures looky-loos back to Winthrop in January of 1933; and gale-force winds smash boats (below) near Weymouth in September of 1936.

What was the lowest barometric pressure reading taken in New England during the Hurricane of 1938?

According to "The Country Journal New England Weather Book," the lowest reading in New England during the devastating storm of Sept. 21, 1938, was recorded in Hartford, Conn., at 28.04 inches of mercury, or 949.5 millibars. But nowhere in New England did the atmospheric pressure fall as low as it did at Bellport, N.Y., where a low of 27.94 inches/946.2 millibars was recorded. In Burlington, Vt., near the end of the storm's path, the low reading was 28.68 inches/971.2 milibars. The greatest loss of life and the greatest amount of damage was caused by the hurricane's tidal surge along the shorelines of Rhode Island and Massachusetts.

What were the highest recorded winds in Boston during Hurricane Hugo in 1989?

The Globe of Sept. 24, the day after the storm swept through this area, reported that the highest winds recorded in Boston were gusts of 47 mph, while peak gusts of 55 mph were reported in Augusta, Maine. Hugo's last gasps knocked down trees and caused hundreds of power outages across New England, but the storm did not bring the heavy rains that had been expected.

1938

(SEPT. 21)
Even after the wind and sea began to batter the coast on Sept. 21, 1938, New Englanders didn't quite grasp that the storm of the century was upon them. The region hadn't had a hurricane in more than 100 years, only some "great gales" in the 1800s, and people were just expecting heavy rain. But in four and a half hours, a hurricane roared across New York's Long Island and smashed into New England. It was the worst in the region's history, leaving about 600 people dead, 2,000 injured, more than 18,000 buildings destroyed, and billions of dollars in damages. As the full force hit New London, Conn., wind speeds reached 98 mph before the Navy's wind gauges were blown away. Atop the Blue Hill Observatory in Massachusetts, winds of 121 mph and gusts of 186 mph were recorded. Providence, R.I., was flooded as tides surged more than 13 feet above normal. The storm — officially nameless but popularly dubbed the "Long Island Express," the "(Great) New England Hurricane," or the "Great Hurricane of '38" — put pressure on Congress to fund hurricane research and more advanced warning systems that would prove vital in years to come.

Downtown Providence under water.

MEET THE
Meteorologist

Don Kent

**LEGENDARY
WEATHERCASTER, NOW
RETIRED IN NEW HAMPSHIRE**

On Sept. 21, 1938, the Boston Weather Bureau was forecasting just a big rainstorm in New England. But I saw the storm as a dangerous hurricane — the first big New England hurricane in about 100 years.

I still have vivid memories of how that storm looked at its height between 5 and 6 p.m. I was nearly 21 years old at the time and I remember standing on Quincy Shore Drive in Quincy, Mass., with my parents and brother when the entire roof of the Wollaston Yacht Club blew into the sea.

A 70-foot yacht tossed ashore at Onset, Mass.

People needing people in 1938: A girl finds no shortage of gallant rescuers in Hartford, Conn. (above), while help arrives by rowboat in East Hartford (far right). And sitting down is the only way to take in the damage at home in Highland Park, R.I. (right).

1944

(SEPT. 15) Memories of the 1938 blast were still fresh when a Category 3 blockbuster moved with ferocious speed up the Eastern Seaboard from Sept. 14-15, 1944. Lost at sea in the "Great Atlantic Hurricane" were five ships at a cost of more than 300 lives. On shore, 46 people died. Fortunately, the storm's center missed Boston, veering northeast to pass by Portland, Rockland, and Bar Harbor, Maine. This time, newly hurricane-conscious New Englanders were prepared; they had also been conducting wartime bomb and blackout drills. But while areas such as New Bedford, Mass., and Cape Cod were hit even harder than in 1938, the region generally took less of a beating. German prisoners of war were put to work in the after-storm cleanup, including picking windfall fruit from the area's ruined apple crop.

The hurricane's high winds take a toll on Bay State Road in Boston (left) and at the Hyannisport Beach Club on Cape Cod (above).

MEET THE
Meteorologist

Dick Albert
WCVB-TV, BOSTON, MASS.

I spent hours and hours as a child observing the ocean in Ogunquit, Maine, where my family vacationed. We were there on Aug. 31, 1954, when the winds were picking up rapidly in fitful gusts; Hurricane Carol was heading up the coast at breakneck speed.

The urge to get outside was overwhelming for a 10-year-old boy, so I snuck outside where the winds were howling, the trees were swaying, and branches were falling all around me. The ocean was a blanket of white foam and gigantic waves.

Barely able to stand up against the winds, I somehow managed to make it home unscathed. It was a very dangerous thing to do and my parents were not happy, but I'll never forget that day.

Above: Soldiers man a short-wave radio in Hyannis, Mass.

Left: Carol's wreckage includes houses, a trailer park, and a bridge (left center) crossing Route 1 off Block Island Sound.

1954

(AUG. 31) New England received tumultuous visits from two devastating "girls," Carol and Edna, within two weeks of each other. In 1954 New Englanders were still getting used to the new policy established by the National Weather Service of giving a woman's name to individual tropical storms. Carol, the first major named storm, raced into New England on the morning of Aug. 31, 1954, hitting Boston with 100 mph gusts that toppled the steeple of the Old North Church. The Category 3 blow took at least 60 lives. Maine's apple crop was cut in half; the state's fishermen and lobstermen suffered a $1 million loss.

MEET THE
Meteorologist

John Ghiorse
WJAR-TV, PROVIDENCE, R.I.

My father, a high school physics teacher, was a bit of a weather nut. He had a dog-eared atlas that he'd drag out every time a hurricane was spotted in the tropics. We'd strain to pick up coordinates through the hisses and whistles emanating from his short-wave radio receiver, and then we'd plot its location on the map of the Atlantic Ocean. In late August of 1954, Hurricane Carol was at 34.2N, 76.1W, nearing Cape Hatteras with sustained winds topping 100 mph.

After a restless night's sleep, we were up at the crack of dawn and low clouds were moving fast. Pretty soon shingles rattled on the backside of our house in Braintree, Mass., and when I looked out I saw bricks flicking off the neighbor's chimney. Trees staggered and toppled in a gust like candlepins struck by a giant bowling ball. I was scared, yet at the same time exhilarated.

It took another eight years or so before I could technically call myself a meteorologist, but it was on that summer day in 1954 that I knew I was really hooked.

"*Having the eye pass over was the most magical thing of all. Suddenly the air was milky warm and eerily calm. Suddenly the sky was blue ... Kids popped out of houses. ... We did a little rain dance, and sure enough the rain began again.*"

CAROL STOCKER, Globe Staff and native Rhode Islander, writing about Hurricane Carol

After the hurricane: WBZ-TV's toppled broadcasting tower in Brighton, Mass., and an al fresco meal (left) at Swift's Beach in Wareham, Mass.

(SEPT. 11) Eleven days after Carol hit, the even more powerful Edna slammed into Massachusetts on Sept. 11, 1954, with gusts of up to 120 mph. Another 20 lives were lost. Together the storms tallied millions of dollars in clean-up costs. Stoic New Englanders contented themselves by saying the double-blast was bad, but not as bad as the Hurricane of 1938.

In Massachusetts, authorities stand watch (above left) as a Barnstable boater navigates the waters of Hurricane Edna and helpful boys pump out the basement of a flooded Worcester liquor store (above).

**How are hurricane categories
defined, and where does the
word "hurricane" come from?**

Category 1 means a
tropical storm has sustained
(one minute) wind speed
ranging from 74 to 95 miles
per hour. The range for a
Category 2 is 96 to 110 miles
per hour; for Category 3, it's
111 to 130; for Category 4,
it's 131 to 155; and for
Category 5, the so-called
"catastrophic storm," it's
anything 156 and above.
According to the National
Weather Service's National
Hurricane Center, the word
for these tropical storms is
derived from "Hurican," the
Carib god of evil, whose
name in turn was derived
from the Mayan god
Hurakan.

**What is the difference between
a hurricane watch and a
hurricane warning?**

A spokesman for the
National Weather Service
office at Logan Airport tells
us a warning means
hurricane conditions are
either imminent or expected
within 24 hours. A watch
means such conditions are
possible within 24 to 36
hours.

(AUGUST) Put two relatively mild hurricanes back to back and the resulting one-two punch will be anything but meek. First, Hurricane Connie soaked the region on Aug. 12 and 13, 1955; then Hurricane Diane arrived. The Category 1 event was a bit of a softy when it moved across Long Island and into east-central Connecticut and Massachusetts on Aug. 17. But the storm lingered through Aug. 19 with record-breaking rain, including 18-plus inches that fell over a 24-hour period in Westfield, Mass. The deluge caused devastating floods with widespread collapses of dams and bridges. The toll was 90 deaths and millions of dollars in property losses.

During and after: The Blackstone River in Pawtucket, R.I., roiling from Hurricane Diane (far left) and then back to normal two weeks later (left).

1955

ASK THE *Globe*

When did the practice begin of naming hurricanes?

In the written history of the Caribbean, the naming of really bad hurricanes goes back at least to the early 19th century when they were named for the saint's day on which they struck. By the end of the 19th century, Australian meteorologist Clement Wragge had devised a new naming system using ordinary female names for tropical storms in the Pacific (typhoons). The US National Weather Service adopted this practice in 1953. Then, in 1978, men's names were added for typhoons and, in 1979, men's names were also introduced for hurricanes in the Atlantic and Gulf of Mexico. The names are selected by the World Meteorological Organization in Geneva, which rotates lists and also retires the names of exceptionally damaging storms.

How long does hurricane season last?

The Atlantic hurricane season nominally begins in June, reaches its peak in September, and ends in November. More than 100 disturbances with hurricane potential are spotted and recorded each year in the Atlantic Ocean, the Caribbean Sea, and the Gulf of Mexico. However, only about 10 attain the status of tropical storm (sustained winds of 39 mph or more) and only about six become hurricanes (sustained winds of at least 74 mph).

(SEPT. 12-13) Donna was a storm with staying power. The Category 3 event mauled Puerto Rico, causing 107 deaths, before attacking the North American mainland from Sept. 12 to 13, 1960. Donna was the only hurricane on record to produce hurricane-force winds in Florida and the mid-Atlantic states as well as New England. Before this storm's fury eased, 50 more people on the mainland were dead.

Donna lands in the Bay State: Flooding Falmouth Heights (left) and parts of Worcester (previous page), and downing power lines in Dartmouth (above).

1976

(AUG. 10) On Aug. 9, 1976, the small hamlet of West Wardsboro, Vt., had only one street. By 6:30 p.m. on Aug. 10, it had none. When Hurricane Belle hit New England, southern Vermont took the brunt of the storm with 6 inches of rain that sent hundreds scrambling for higher ground. West Wardsboro was engulfed by the nearby creek, leaving the town in ruins. The flooding seriously damaged crops, including hay — a mainstay of the state's dairy industry.

Belle's destructive shower of tree limbs in Milford, Mass.

MEET THE
Meteorologist

Ken Barlow
WBZ-TV, BOSTON, MASS.

When Hurricane Belle was threatening in 1976, I remember staying up all night in Newport, R.I., watching and waiting for the storm to move up the East Coast. I was 16 years old and it was the first real test of my meteorological future: Would I still be excited about a career in weather if the loss of sleep wasn't worth it?

I fought off fatigue and made it through the night. In the morning, trees were down everywhere and boulders closed Newport's Memorial Boulevard. The surf was the highest I had ever seen it at Easton's Beach.

The storm was all I thought it would be, so I stuck to my plan and stuck with weather. I haven't been disappointed yet.

MEET THE
Meteorologist

Brian Lapis
WWLP-TV, CHICOPEE, MASS.

Hurricane Gloria whipped through our area of eastern Connecticut in what seemed only a couple of hours and with little damage to our home and property, but we were without power for a week. I was in high school at the time and I recall that was when I first developed an appreciation for the power that weather has to rearrange our lives. Now I worry about what problems a significant hurricane could bring.

Kelly Bates
WJAR-TV, PROVIDENCE, R.I.

When I was a child growing up in North Attleboro, Mass., Hurricane Gloria taught me about the raw power of nature. I remember the frequency of the thunderstorms, and all of the radio stations playing that old song, "Gloria," in between storm updates. Most of all, I remember the wind.

We had a large weeping willow tree in the front yard that groaned closer to our house with each gust. Just when we thought it was going to let go, the winds stopped and the sky cleared. It was remarkable to see how nature could be so fierce one moment, and then so serene. Hurricane Gloria is the reason I chose weather as my career.

1985

(SEPT. 27) Radio stations had a field day playing versions of the 1964 Van Morrison classic, "Gloria," when forecasters predicted that Hurricane Gloria was headed for the East Coast. Gloria ambled along the Atlantic Coast and hit land in Connecticut the morning of Sept. 27, 1985, moving swiftly through Rhode Island, Massachusetts, New Hampshire, and parts of Maine. The storm's 100-mph winds downed power lines, pummeled apple crops, and caused eight deaths. But Gloria proved to be a lady with much less power than first predicted.

First, ominous clouds hang over Boston (previous page), then Hurricane Gloria's fury is felt in the Massachusetts communities of Winthrop (above left), New Bedford (left), and Falmouth (above).

A pedestrian hangs in the wind on Boston's St. James Street during Hurricane Bob.

1991

(AUG. 19) Even with weather satellites, radar, and computer modeling systems, Hurricane Bob was a shock. That's because Bob formed off the Bahamas, well north of the usual spawning ground of hurricanes, and moved with unusual speed toward the East Coast, reaching hurricane force only when it was already nearing the Carolinas. New Englanders barely had time to take notice before they were hit on Aug. 19, 1991 with 100 mph winds and torrential rains. Gusts reached 125 mph on Rhode Island's Block Island. Fortunately, Bob passed through and into Canadian waters with equally swift speed, but the storm still wracked up more than $900 million in damage during its sprint. Five days later, thousands of people on Cape Cod were still without electricity.

Why doesn't the government bomb the eye of a hurricane to change its path?

According to Robert Sheets, former head of the federal National Hurricane Center, nothing can have any significant impact on a hurricane, even at its formative stage. "The amount of energy released in the average hurricane in a 24-hour period is equivalent to the explosion of more than 400 20-megaton bombs," he says. These storm systems cover tens of thousands of square miles even at their earliest stages and draw their energy from the ocean over hundreds of thousands of square miles.

How does the dew point relate to humidity?

The dew point is the temperature at which moist air reaches saturation and water vapor begins to condense. Relative humidity is 100 percent when the dew point is the same as the air temperature. For example, when the dew point is 65 degrees and the air temperature is 65 degrees, relative humidity is 100 percent. Or, if the air temperature is 80 degrees and the dew point is 65 degrees, you would need to cool the air mass by 15 degrees to reach 100 percent humidity.

Bob's boat bash in Dartmouth, Mass.

A not-so-perfect storm for Bay State residents in Revere (above) and Hull (right).

(OCT. 30) The storm that never got an official name is now one of New England's most famous. Right from the start it was highly unusual; it emerged out of a low-pressure system in Canada and moved southwest, a track that amplified the force of its counterclockwise winds. When this "No-Name Storm" reached the Atlantic, it merged with the dwindling remains of Hurricane Grace, a lethal combination that author Sebastian Junger called "The Perfect Storm." It hit New England full force on Oct. 30, 1991; by mid-afternoon 30-foot waves were crashing onto the North and South shores of Massachusetts Bay, smashing homes and washing away piers and beaches. Offshore, winds reached 81 mph and created 43-foot waves. The six-man crew of the Andrea Gail fishing boat out of Gloucester, Mass., was lost; their story is chronicled in Junger's bestseller and a subsequent Hollywood film.

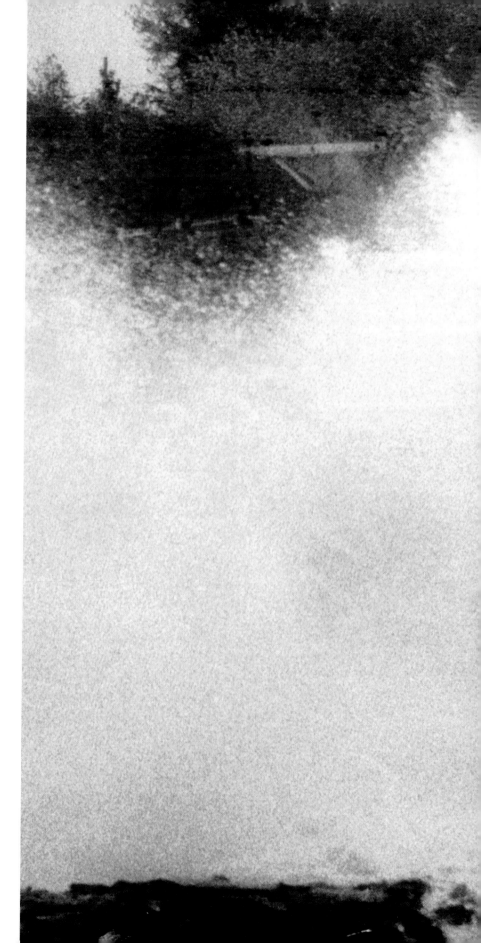

MEET THE
Meteorologist

Al Kaprielian
MYTV NEW ENGLAND,
DERRY N.H.

Anyone who lives by the Atlantic Ocean knows that weather can intensify quickly and chart its own unique course.

In the "No-Name Storm" (a.k.a. "The Perfect Storm") of October 1991, a cold front stalled offshore. A low-pressure system formed on the front and this low merged with Hurricane Grace into one powerful storm.

An omega block formed in the jet stream; when this block forms, the normal west-to-east movement of weather stops. A reverse occurs when storms out at sea can retrograde (back in). This is what happened with the No-Name Storm: it backed in from the ocean, with strong offshore winds causing surges that flooded many roads.

Posing for pictures on a Chatham, Mass., dock during the glancing blow of 1996's Hurricane Edouard. Nobody made a Hollywood blockbuster out of this one.

120

Tourists hit Hull, Mass., to view remnants of Hurricane Edouard on Sept. 2, 1996.

On Cape Cod, Edouard snaps power lines along Route 132 (left) and whips up sand on a Chatham beach (below).

FLOODS

It should come as no surprise that New England, with its snow-catching mountains and numerous major rivers, has had its share of flood disasters.

In November of 1927, more than 80 people died as excessive waters rampaged down the White and Winooski rivers in Vermont, where residents were forced to flee onto roofs and into trees.

The events of March 1936 remain particularly momentous for New Englanders. Vast stretches of the region, including Hartford, Conn., and Manchester, N.H., were under water. The widespread destruction prompted major improvements in flood control.

Connecticut's other momentous soakers include a dam-busting event in June of 1982. Maine had an April Fools' Day in 1987 that saw rivers rise more than 20 feet. And Bostonians surely remember October of '96, when sections of the city's subway system were knocked out of service for days as rain sent water gushing into tunnels and stations.

What is a hurricane for seaside residents can cause major flooding for folks inland. We leave it to others to debate and categorize. The upshot is water, water everywhere.

Many people don't believe there was a big molasses spill that caused several deaths [not storm-related, but still among the most fascinating floods in American history]. Can you enlighten them?

At about noon on Jan. 15, 1919, a huge tank holding 2.3 million gallons of raw molasses burst a seam and sent a wave of the sticky syrup, up to 30 feet high in the beginning, over several blocks in Boston's North End. The fast-flowing wave of goop trapped and killed 21 people. Another 150 people were injured. The weather was exceptionally mild that day and the tragedy at first was blamed on the rapid expansion of the molasses. An official investigation, however, uncovered problems in the construction of the tank at the Purity Distilling Co. The company was ordered to pay more than $1 million in damages.

What is the significance of the colored and sometimes flashing lights on top of the old John Hancock building?

The light system of weather forecasting on the John Hancock building has been put to rhyme to make it easier to remember: Steady blue, clear view; flashing blue, clouds due; steady red, rain ahead; flashing red, snow instead.

A Harvard Square (Cambridge, Mass.) cemetery after severe rains in 1926.

127

1927

Vermont under water: A bridge bowing to Mother Nature in Bellows Falls (above),
a Rochester home in trouble (above right), and train travel hampered at Bellows Falls (bottom right).

(NOV. 3-4) It's considered the single worst natural disaster in Vermont
history. The two-day deluge of up to 10 inches of rain that fell on
Nov. 3-4 in 1927 caused at least 84 deaths, including the drowning of the
state's lieutenant governor, S. Hollister Jackson. The White and Winooski
rivers overflowed and surging waters coming on the heels of a very wet
October destroyed more than 1,000 bridges in addition to acres of roads,
railroad tracks, houses, and crops.

Rescuing New England flood victims, exact location and fate unknown.

1936

(MARCH) "No such widespread wave of destruction has swept over New England in the memory of living men," The Boston Globe solemnly reported after massive floods swept away homes, businesses, farms, and lives throughout five states in March of 1936. It was no exaggeration. The disaster spread from the mountains of New Hampshire to the valleys of Connecticut in a single merciless month. It began with unrelenting torrential rains throughout the region: 20 plus inches in Pinkham Notch between March 1 and 20. Rivers quickly swelled to overflowing; the Merrimack, the Connecticut, and the Kennebec burst their banks, turning the countryside into lakes. Walls of water brought down icepacks from the mountains, which smashed dams and bridges. Entire homes were swept downstream. Manchester, N.H., and Hartford, Conn., were among cities submerged in several feet of water. By the third week of March, the region's river valleys were sprawling disaster areas; as many as 100,000 people were displaced and about 100 deaths were recorded. Today a vast network of flood control reservoirs, dams, and dikes has been designed to prevent the reoccurrence of such destructive flooding.

Swept away by 1938 flood waters in Ware, Mass.

MEET THE
Meteorologist

Geoff Fox
**WTNH-TV,
NEW HAVEN, CONN.**

I have a weather fear. I suspect it's a common worry of meteorologists: I'm petrified of a repeat of the Great Hurricane of 1938.

That storm's surge, 17 feet above a normal high tide, drove flooding waters into downtown Providence. Hartford saw the Connecticut River rise to 19 feet above flood stage, and 50-foot waves crashed at Gloucester, Mass.

Today, we have the advantage of satellites, radar, and high-speed computers. But hurricanes remain difficult to predict. Another event like the storm of '38 (more on page 88), which moved from the Bahamas to New England in little more than a day, could overwhelm us. Would we try and evacuate the entire East Coast?

All I know is the scenario has happened before. It will happen again.

1938

A washout day
for Boston-area
roller skaters,
who can't get
past abnormally
high tides
in December
of 1959.

Above: Wading through several inches of rainwater on Boston's Charles Street in 1960.

Left: An appropriate marquee for the situation in 1959 at the Park Theatre in Worcester, Mass.

135

> **"We live in a time in our country and the world when it seems weather catastrophes are more common. We now have 100-year floods every two years, it seems."**
>
> AL GORE, touring Maine as vice president in 1998

In January of 1979, a motorist abandons her stalled car in high waters on Front Street in Worcester, Mass.

In June of 1982, a Mercedes negotiates Worcester's flooded Central Street.

(JUNE 5-6) One of the worst storms in a century hit Connecticut on June 5, 1982, when the state was drenched with up to a foot of rain over a 24-hour period. The constant downpour broke a series of dams that sent water into the overflowing Falls River and created a four-mile swath of damage in southern Connecticut. Swollen rivers washed out roads, bridges, and dams, and disrupted electricity, telephone services, and public transportation. About 150 families were left homeless and 10 deaths were recorded. They included a 62-year-old woman who was rescued from her stalled car in Lyme by a town highway crew; she was killed when the crew's truck fell off a collapsed bridge.

MEET THE
Meteorologist

Mark Searles
WLNE-TV, PROVIDENCE, R.I.

I've had the pleasure of working alongside some of the most established and experienced meteorologists in southern New England. Fortunately for me, each one has passed along his or her unique styles and concepts, many of which I call upon on a daily basis. The one lesson they have all relayed has been this: Just when you think you have the weather patterns of southern New England figured out, invariably something happens to throw your confidence right out the window.

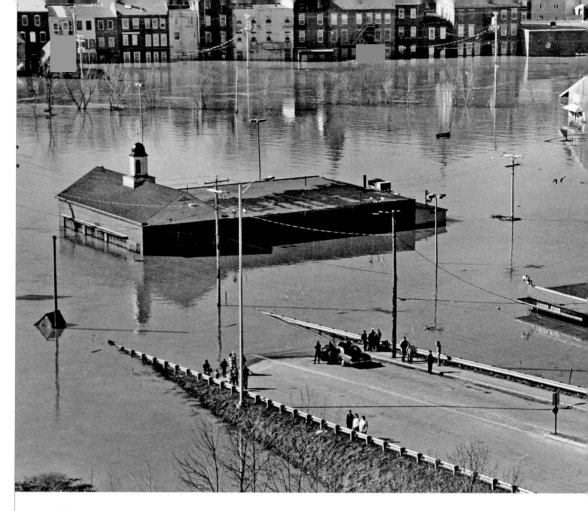

The Kennebec River engulfs a road and shopping mall in Gardner, Maine (April 2, 1987).

1987

(APRIL 1) The catastrophic flood hit on April Fools' Day 1987, causing serious damage to businesses and homes along Maine's major waterways. Rivers rose more than 20 feet in less than a day and swept away roads, bridges, and historic structures. No deaths were reported, but more than 2,000 Maine homes were flooded and a couple of hundred were destroyed. Sections of small towns were left without power and isolated for days. The Low's Covered Bridge was torn apart as a resident captured the event with his new camera, according to an account in the Bangor Daily News, then he broke down and cried.

1992

An aerial view of Main Street in downtown Montpelier, Vt., on March 11, 1992, when ice jams pushed the Winooski River over its banks.

Has it ever rained frogs?
In his book, "Weather Force," John Gribbin claims that thousands of the amphibians fell to earth during a violent storm in Madras, India, in 1911, and that in 1939 a heavy shower in Wiltshire, England, deposited countless tiny frogs in and around a municipal swimming pool. Gribbin also says there was a shower of snails in Redruth, England, in 1886; he maintains it rained red worms in Sweden in 1924; and he says an alligator was reported to have fallen onto a street in Charleston, S.C., during a severe thunderstorm in 1843.

A soggy, ground-level view of Montpelier's Main Street in 1992.

1996

(OCT. 20-21) Torrential rain fell across New England beginning on Oct. 20, 1996, unleashing widespread flooding that filled basements and washed away roads and bridges. Paradoxically, the flooding left 120,000 Maine residents without water as the storm broke water mains. Clouds dumped 19-plus inches of rain on Camp Ellis in Maine and poured record amounts on New Hampshire. Boston's Green Line subway was knocked out of service for days. In Wells, Maine, snowplows were used to clear seaweed; in Revere, Mass., the plows tackled sand.

Paddling down Shawmut Street in Revere, Mass.

MEET THE
Meteorologist

Mike Haddad
WMUR-TV,
MANCHESTER, NH

The Northeast is one of only two US regions (the Mid-Atlantic states to North Carolina being the other) where each type of major storm can occur. Having forecast all kinds of extreme weather in New Hampshire at the end of the 20th century, one storm that stands out for me is the powerful northeaster of October 1996, which turned streets into rivers and ruined many homes and businesses in the Granite State. This event saw the most rain ever predicted by a computer model for parts of New Hampshire.

But while the 1996 flood was rare and devastating, it could not compare to the sequence of 21st-century events I covered beginning in the fall of 2005, when New Hampshire saw three major floods in only 18 months. The job of forecasting in New England is one of constant anticipation.

Above: Braving a huge puddle on American Legion Highway in Hyde Park, Mass. (Oct. 20, 1996).

Left: A 4-year-old surveys his yard along the swollen Shawsheen River in Billerica, Mass. (Oct. 22, 1996).

MEET THE
Meteorologist

Matt Noyes
NECN, NEWTON, MASS.

As a New Englander, I've always believed that no region offers a more diverse spectacle of nature. As a meteorologist, that belief became conviction.

The unique aura surrounding New England weather isn't just about the air that turns our wind vanes, the clouds obscuring our mountaintops, or the swell churning our ocean waters. Here, we respect the awesome power of the world around us and our vulnerability to its whim. We'll push through whatever nature has to dish out, and the respect that we as a weather-savvy community hold for our cornucopia of conditions is a daily inspiration to meteorologists.

I'm constantly reminded that my responsibility is to reach for perfection and, knowing that's impossible, prepare my neighbors for a range of possibilities. It's a challenge to be met head-on, without fail.

On July 15, 1997, residents of Montgomery, Vt., view what's left of a bridge washed-out by torrential rains and flooding along the Trout River.

1997

1998

(JUNE) One of the soggiest Junes ever recorded in New England happened in 1998, when nearly a foot of rain collected in Boston alone. A witty meteorologist blamed the month's rainfall on a slow-moving, Canada-bound jet stream lingering over the area "like a summer tourist reluctant to go home." Several Vermont counties were declared federal disaster areas; communities along the Mad River were particularly hard hit on June 27 when flood waters wrecked mobile homes, ripped through bridges and roads, and trapped people in trees and on rooftops. In New Hampshire, a man was killed when he was pulled into a culvert he was trying to clear of debris.

Rescue workers pull together in Bristol, Vt., on June 27, 1998.

YOUR PHOTOS

When we asked New Englanders to send in their extreme weather photographs from the 20th century, we got hundreds of submissions. Here are 10 favorites.

To see more entries and to purchase images seen in this book, visit BostonGlobeStore.com/storms

The No-Name Storm (a.k.a. The Perfect Storm) of October 1991 engulfs Winthrop Shore Drive in Winthrop, Mass.
—PHOTO COURTESY OF SY CHERENSON, WINTHROP, MASS.

Boats aground in Stony Creek, Conn., following the Hurricane of 1938. In the foreground is the Tormentor,
washed ashore from its mooring in a small inlet just off Thimble Islands Road.
The other boat farther down the road is the ferry boat, Starlite, washed in from the harbor.

—PHOTO COURTESY OF LORETTA FOX, STONY CREEK, CONN.

The Coast Guard reaches out to help a lobster boat washed up against the shore of Rockland, Maine, during the winter of 1967-'68.
—Photo courtesy of Leo Chabot, North Andover, Mass.

Five days after the Blizzard of 1978,
abandoned cars still squat along Route. 128 in Massachusetts at the Dedham/Westwood line.

−PHOTO COURTESY OF JOE MCDERMOTT
(VP-EMERITUS, BOSTON RED SOX), MEDFIELD, MASS.

State Street in Portland, Maine, is a winter wonderland after a January 1988 snowstorm.
—Photo courtesy of Dan Durloo, Portland, Maine

A building in the Bass Rocks section of Gloucester, Mass., covered in ice by the Blizzard of 1978.

– PHOTO COURTESY OF JOSEPH PELCZARSKI
(REGIONAL PLANNER, COASTAL ZONE MANAGEMENT), BOSTON, MASS.

What's left of the concession stand at Devereux Beach
in Marblehead, Mass.,
following the No-Name Storm of October 1991.
—PHOTO COURTESY OF TOM ADAMS,
MARBLEHEAD, MASS.

A shift in property values on Egypt Beach in Scituate, Mass.,
after the Blizzard of '78.
—PHOTO COURTESY OF STEVE PUCCI,
WEST NEWBURY, MASS.

1938 hurricane destruction at New Silver Beach
in North Falmouth, Mass.
—PHOTO COURTESY OF THOMAS MCGILVRAY,
BOLTON, MASS.

In the wake of the Blizzard of 1978, monster surf provides days of excitement along Winthrop Shore Drive in Winthrop, Mass.
—Photo courtesy of John McLaughlin, Winthrop, Mass.

"One of the brightest gems in the New England weather is the dazzling uncertainty of it."

MARK TWAIN

Fenway Park, June 26, 1997.